LARRY JACOBS

GreenWinter
Celebrations of Old Age

by

Elise Maclay

READER'S DIGEST PRESS
distributed by
Thomas Y. Crowell Company
New York   1977

Manufactured in the United States of America

LIBRARY OF CONGRESS CATALOGING IN PUBLICATION DATA

Maclay, Elise.
  Green winter.

  1. Old age. 2. Aging. I. Title.
HQ1061.M23   301.43'5   76-54239
ISBN 0-88349-122-2

10 9 8 7 6 5 4 3 2 1

This book would not have been written
without my mother's belief in God
and my sons' belief in me.

That in my age as cheerful I might be
As the green winter of the Holly Tree

ROBERT SOUTHEY
The Holly Tree

Acknowledgments

The photographs that appear in *Green Winter* were taken by the following people and may not be reproduced without permission:

Page number   *Photo Credit*
Page iii: Grete Mannheim, dpi
Page 15:   Bob Andrews, dpi
Page 24:   Francis Laping, dpi
Page 40:   John Bacchus, dpi
Page 49:   Henry Street Settlement Urban Life Center
Page 57:   Garrett Browne Gibbs
Page 61:   Lutheran Community Services, Inc.
Page 66:   Lida Moser, dpi
Page 91:   Garrett Browne Gibbs
Page 98:   Ann Griffiths, dpi
Page 103:   Phoebe Dunn, dpi
Page 115:   Bob Andrews, dpi
Page 124:   Henry Monroe, dpi
Page 129:   Susanne, dpi

The material quoted in "For Parents and Poets and the Aurora Borealis" is reprinted by permission of Abigail Van Buren, Chicago Tribune–New York News Syndicate; the material quoted in "Letter to Thomas B. Russiano" is reprinted by permission of Ms. Magazine.

Preface

The word portraits in this book are of real people. But they are not interviews. They are reflections of the spirit of men and women I have known—some over a period of many years, some a shorter time, some for only an instant of intimacy. Like you, like me, these men, these women, were not, are not, always as they appear here—rejoicing, despairing, taking new heart. But these are the particular moments to which I was granted entrance. I recorded them because they are precious, and worthy of being preserved and shared. But they are not unique. Wisdom, courage, insights, commonality shimmer around us if we have the heart to see beyond the cataract-clouded eye, the shaking hand, the slipped-mooring memory.

Anyone could have written this book. Anyone can write a book like it. The references—and points of reference—walk a little way ahead of all of us who are not yet old, saying with their breath and being and our shared humanness (although their words seem to be about other things), "We are you later on."

The photographs are not illustrations of the text but different impressions of old age, come upon independently.

xiii

Contents

THE COURAGE OF FRIENDS
What a new face courage puts on everything! (Ralph Waldo Emerson)

LOOKING UP
*But they that wait upon the Lord shall renew
their strength (Isaiah 40:31)*

Green Winter

Assessing and Defining

Within I do not find weariness and used heart, but unspent youth.

RALPH WALDO EMERSON

My Children
Are Coming Today

My children are coming today. They mean well. But they
worry.

They think I should have a railing in the hall. A telephone
in the kitchen. They want someone to come in when I
take a bath.

They really don't like my living alone.

Help me to be grateful for their concern. And help them to
understand that I have to do what I can as long as I
can.

They're right when they say there are risks. I might fall. I
might leave the stove on. But there is no challenge, no
possibility of triumph, no real aliveness without risk.

When they were young and climbed trees and rode bicy-
cles and went away to camp, I was terrified. But I let
them go.

Because to hold them would have hurt them.

Now our roles are reversed. Help them see.

Keep me from being grim or stubborn about it. But don't
let me let them smother me.

I Keep Forgetting Things

I keep forgetting things:
Which letters I've answered,
Whether I turned the stove off.
But I keep remembering things, too:
Faces, places,
Sights, scents, sounds.
It's annoying not to know where I left my glasses,
But it's lovely to have always, right behind my eyes,
A picture of my daughter at three,
Hair glinting in the sun,
Looking up at me,
Asking: "Do butterflies have puppies or is it the other way
    around?"
I can recall perfectly the sound of a fog horn
Off the coast of Maine,
Though, as the family will tell you,
I sometimes don't hear the phone.
I remember graduations and weddings and
Picnics and parades,
The way a fresh-cut lawn smells,
The taste of apricot jam.
Help me to be happy about what I remember
Instead of fretting about what I forget.
I'd rather relive love than find my glasses.
(But, of course, Lord, I wouldn't mind if you wanted to
    give me a hint.)

Carpenter

I like to make things out of wood.
The older I get, the stronger I build.
Am I trying to build immortality?
I don't think so.
I know that whether I live or die
The things I make have a life of their own,
Separate and apart.
I just want them to have a good life
And long,
Like I've had.
Thanks, God, for building me strong.

Teacher

God, how cruel your creatures are!
I have a friend who teaches art,
Free,
At the Civic Center,
Faithfully,
Though she's in her seventies
And has arthritis.
Recently she had to go to the hospital,
She left assignments, lessons, plans.
When she came back, one of her pupils said,
"Look what we did without you—
This and this and this—
We don't need you."
My friend said, "That's wonderful.
You know, that's the nicest thing a
Teacher can hear.
I'm proud to know
I taught you so well you can go on
Without me."
O God, how wise and cheerful and unresentful
Your creatures are!

I Miss Being Needed

I miss being needed.
Once the whole family depended on me.
I was the breadwinner.
Only I didn't *win* the bread, I worked hard and earned it.
When I picked up my paycheck, I was proud.
I didn't mind that it went for the family.
I was proud to buy shoes, a Flexible Flyer sled, a college
    education.
I was needed at work.
In the community.
At home.
To build and haul.
To serve on committees.
To decide things. To help people out.
Sometimes I'd get exasperated and say, Does the whole
    world have to lean on me?
Now I wish somebody would.
The trouble is, now that I'm old, people have no idea what
    I'm good for.
Well, neither do I.
But I can find out.
Maybe to be needed, a man doesn't always have to be
    doing something. He can just be there. Like a star. A
    fixed point. For others to take their bearings from.

Infirmities

In line, in the supermarket,
I stood next to a young woman with a baby.
The baby drooled,
His mother smiled and wiped his mouth with a tissue.
The baby seized the tissue and threw it to the floor.
His mother picked it up, laughing.
He grabbed it again and threw it under our feet.
Again and again.
His mother laughed.
The baby squirmed, disarranged his clothes,
Grew red in the face,
Babbled gibberish.
His mother cuddled him and smiled.
Would she be so gentle,
So understanding, so kind,
To an old father, trembling, murmuring,
Wandering in his mind?
Am I? To my friends who falter and fail.
Why do the infirmities of age revolt us?
They seem unnatural.
We're wrong; all living things move gently toward decay.
Is a blasted oak revolting?
Are we afraid? Yes. I draw inwardly away
From my failing friends because I see
Myself in them. I don't drool,
But tomorrow I may. My hands shake

And I don't always catch what people say.
Help us to be as gentle with old people
As we are with infants.
Help us to look past the tic, the tremor, the gray
Failed flesh the way
We look past the baby's helplessness to see
A unique self
Reflecting Your divinity.

I Miss My Husband

The pain is as sharp and deep as the day he died. People think because I can speak of him calmly, sometimes with a smile, that I am over it. You don't love that much and live that close and get over it. Ever. Sometimes I hurt so much I want to run to someone, be held fast, have my head stroked. But he is the one I would have run to. His arms would have held me, his hands stroked my head. Now there is no one. No comfort. Only pain.

> *My peace I give unto you,*
> *Not as the world giveth . . .*

Where did those words come from? Out of my subconscious? From you? And what is that sound? A bird? Are you trying to tell me that your comfort is different? I don't understand and I do. In some inexplicable way there *is* comfort in the inexorable return of the birds. In the reliability of dawn. In the warmth of the sun.

I miss my husband so much. Thank you for letting me talk about it.

Thank you for talking to me.

Thanks Just the Same

I'm sorry, God,
But I'm not going to live with my son.
He's a good boy,
And I like the girl he married,
And the grandchildren
Are grand children,
But I like walking to the diner
At five thirty in the morning
To have coffee with the truckers.
I like coming home when I want to,
Right away or not till afternoon or night.
I like wearing holey socks or none
Till I get around to stitching them up,
Which all us old Navy men can,
Only I just might never.
Never mind, they're *my* toes
Stickin' through,
My business if they're cold.
I'm old enough to decide
What I want to bother about.
They worry about my "unregulated life."
What's it gonna do?
Stunt my growth?
Make me die sooner?
Okay. I'm ready to go.

I'm also happy to stay.
I'm just not ready to be looked after,
Taken care of, tended to,
Except easy-like, from away off,
By You.

To Be or Not to Be

So many of my friends are gone,
It's as if I were once part of a forest
And now I'm a lone tree
That has withstood a lot of storms
And may or may not
Withstand the next one.
But it's not up to me.
I find that comforting, God.
I'd hate the job of deciding whether
To be or not to be,
At this stage of the game.
I have my up times and my down
And what I decided would depend on
How I felt at the moment.
And I certainly don't have all the facts.
How do I know if I'm through here
Or if there's more for me to do?
When I was younger I was big on
    "running my own life."
(Tried to run quite a few other people's lives, too—Forgive
        me for that.)
Now I'm quite content to let You
    make the major decisions.
Funny thing. I know whenever you call me,
I won't be ready to go,
But that's life. Or should I say death?

Dreams

I seem to be missing some dreams, God.
I almost feel like calling the Lost and Found
Because I had a lot of dreams around here,
Just the other day.
No, a month ago.
No, a year ago.
No, years ago.
Where did they go?
Those dreams.
It sure feels queer without them.
Without something cooking.
That's the way I used to be,
Always into some crackpot scheme,
Always some dream or other
Simmering away on the back burner.
Now, somehow, the old dreams have all sort of petered
    out.
I don't need a lot of dreams, God,
But could You let me have
One or two?

Dieting

This is ridiculous, God,
Dieting to be thin.
I've done it most of my life
With varying degrees of success.
(Success being losing a pound or two, failure being the
    opposite.)
I thought *of* it all the time.
(It got so I couldn't really enjoy putting anything
Except black coffee into my mouth.)
At the same time,
I didn't really think *about* it,
Never stopped to ask,
For whom am I doing
this and why?
When I finally did get around to asking those questions,
The answer was painfully clear.
We females do it because we are like Pavlovian dogs.
When society rings a bell, we conform.
Actually, society has built a great golden idol
Called Media,
And at the sound of the electronic bleep
We, the public, bow down.
Well, You had something to say about that.
And it certainly can't be Your divine will
That we all look like Vogue models
Or the White Rock Girl

16 |

(Who, I recently discovered, has over the years been
    shedding
Draperies and avoirdupois. When you clear the hurdle,
    they raise the bar.)
No. You gave us bodies to use and enjoy
And preserve for those purposes,
And it certainly isn't preserving to fast all day
And eat a Chocolate Milky Way at night,
Which I just did, trying to lose three pounds
Picked up in the course of a four-day, chicken-and-cake
    wedding.
Of course, You don't want us to be fat.
But the emphasis ought to be eating for health:
Energy, stamina, strength,
And if that means wearing a size twelve instead of a size
    eight,
So be it.
Nowhere is it written,
Thou shalt not weigh more than 102.
Male and female You created them.
Also tall and short, big-boned and small,
Wraiths and earth-mothers,
All needing nourishment to bloom,
Fresh vegetables and fruits,
Proteins, whole grain cereals and bread.
Sure, it's a bother to cook when you live alone,
But it's more of a bother to be weak and sick.
And it may be some kind of a sin.
You did, after all, speak of the body as a temple.
Help me to do a better maintenance job.

Don't Let Me
Lose My Sense of Humor

It seems to me I used to laugh more.
Was the world funnier in those days? Of course not. It was
 the same mixture of darkness and light, sadness and
 silliness, doom and delight, then as now, and I used
 to get a lot of laughs out of it. Things haven't
 changed as much as I have. In fact, now that I stop to
 think about it, a lot of the things that annoy me nowadays
 are the same things that used to tickle my funnybone.
Do you heal funnybones, God?
Of course you do.
And the idea
Makes me smile.

Shaving

It's amazing, God,
How wrong a person can be.
Take me and the way
I used to blame old guys for getting seedy-looking.
I used to notice it a lot
When I was young and superior.
I used to think,
At least they could give themselves a close shave,
Don't they care how they look?
Pressed pants and shined shoes don't mean a thing.
Then one day last week, it came to me,
Those guys are shaving without their glasses on.
I used to all the time,
Then this one time last week,
Don't ask me why,
I happened to put my glasses on first.
I hadn't seen my face that close for years.
Wrinkles, hairs, pores.
Stared in the mirror so long
My daughter called upstairs
Was I all right?
I decided
To stop jumping to conclusions
And shaving without my glasses on.
Of course, I might

Grow a beard.
That's the good thing about life, God,
Generally, You offer a couple of alternatives.

Bad Habits

Every time I get rid of a bad habit,
I pick up a new one.
I stopped smoking and started eating
Too many sweets.
I stopped drinking and started watching
Too much TV.
If You were less than divine,
You'd have given up on me.
If anybody doubts Your forgiveness and generosity,
I can submit proof of it:
Me.

Recovery

Well, I'm home from the hospital,
I can eat and drink and smoke.
They took out half my insides,
And my kids, my friends, and the fellows down at the
    bank
Were positive I was going to croak,
And You and I know, God, so was I.
Evidently You have other plans for me.
I can't imagine what they can be,
But I figure if and when You want me to know,
I'll find out.

Money

God, You'd think by now I'd have lived long enough to
    have figured out
How I really feel about money.
Sometimes I think it's everything,
Power and safety,
Peace and happiness.
What dazzling things it can do.
How helpless we feel without it,
At everyone's mercy.
Then something happens
That I can't buy my way out of:
Biopsy. Is it cancer or not?
No news of my son.
Is he alive or dead?
Or I receive a wonderful gift
Which has nothing to do with money:
A sunset. A letter.
My daughter-in-law's love.
Then money seems inconsequential.
It's disconcerting to be seesawing back and forth like this.
When I was young, I thought,
By the time I'm seventy, I'll have things sorted out.
I'll know what matters and what doesn't and how much.
Well, I'm seventy and I'm still weighing and sorting.
Is that good or bad?
I have a feeling it's par for the course.

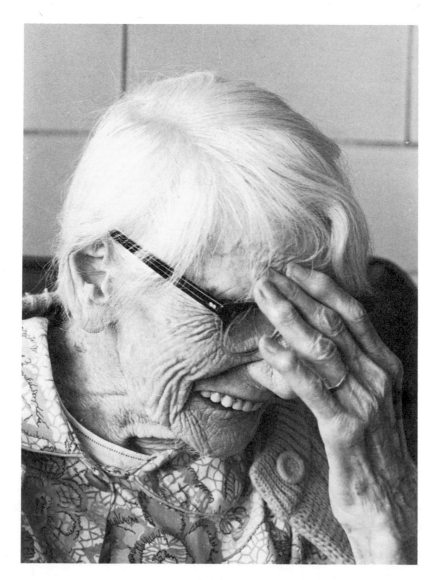

Vanity

I used to hate it so
When a new wrinkle appeared,
Creasing my forehead,
Dragging down my mouth,
Marring my cheek.
I used to sit in front of the mirror
Stretching the skin taut with my fingers,
I could lift it and smooth it,
Which didn't make me feel better,
It made me feel worse,
Remembering how beautiful I used to be.
Well, pretty.
But lately, for almost a year, maybe,
Looking in the mirror hasn't been such a shock.
Am I getting used to it?
Am I reconciled?
Has the deterioration slowed?
No. I need new glasses.
What a joke.
My eyesight's deteriorating faster than my face.
Are You trying to tell me something?
I think so. You said it once:
For everything there is a season.
Old age is not the season for vanity.
Primping took a lot of time.

| 25

If You have freed me from it, You must mean for me
To spend my time on
More appropriate business.

I Said No Today

I said no today.
It took me three days to work up to it.
I talked myself into it
And out of it
Half a dozen times.
"Come on, now," I said to myself,
"It won't hurt you to baby-sit one weekend."
(Of course, it isn't one weekend,
In fact, you could say,
It's getting to be a habit.)
They're adorable, my grandchildren,
And I love them dearly,
But they're messy and noisy
And it makes me nervous to be responsible.
Last week Kim got hold of a breadknife,
I thought she was asleep so I let myself
Doze off a little, too.
Luckily, nothing happened, but it scared me,
That big shining blade.
Of course, it's silly to mind the mess,
It can all be put straight again.
Jimmy broke one of my cobalt cups,
And I doubt if I can mend it, but are things
More important than people?
Of course not.
Still, I do love the look of a neat room.

Sometimes when I'm alone here
With everything dusted and polished and
In its right place,
I just sit and look and smile,
It's so peaceful,
Such a joy,
After years of family life,
Sweaters on the piano,
Tools on the drainboard,
And hardly anything the way
I really wanted it.
Burt was big on convenience,
So the living room was full of end tables
And ash trays, matches and magazines,
A stack of old newspapers for kindling fires.
Of course, you had to leave a bed of ashes on the hearth
And the flu open.
For convenience.
So when a draft blew down the chimney, ashes blew
All over the rug.
His desk was in the living room, too,
And it was always a mess.
I wanted to stand my painted French screen in front,
But he wouldn't have it,
Said he wanted his things handy.
Well, he was a good man,
And he brought a lot into my life, as well,
So I didn't complain.
I'm not complaining now,
Just thinking about how
Exciting it is

To have things the way I want them,
What a pleasure to see
Counters and tabletops clean, clear and free
Of clutter, the way I'd like my life to be
Now.
All my life I've been cluttering up my life
With obligations,
Trying to be
A good daughter, wife, mother, grandmother.
Now
I'd like to pare down, strip away, see
What a day, a week, a month would be
Alone with You,
Alone with me.

Doorman

I'm a doorman, so people talk to me.
They ask me when am I going to retire.
I tell them when I'm six feet under.
Oh, I get tired. Back gets to killing me,
Hands shake.
Still, when I'm laid off sick, time drags.
Not working, it's hard to think up things to fill the day.
Working's better.
Like they say,
Plenty of time to rest
When they put you in that long narrow box.
I'll lie plenty still then,
Unless
You have other plans for me,
Which I sure hope You do.
St. Peter's a fine gatekeeper, I'm sure,
But if he wants some time off
I've been a doorman forty-two years
And I like the work.

My Friend Emily Talks

My friend Emily talks
Whether or not she has anything to say;
She goes on and on.
People keep away from that old chatterbox.
Even her son, I think, makes up excuses
Not to come and see her.
But Emily wasn't always a chatterer.
Married at seventeen, she was a tall, strong, quiet girl,
Practical. More for canning peaches than for reading
    books,
Widowed with a baby at twenty-two,
She took her crippled father-in-law in and cared for him
All his life; he adored her till the day he died.
She did for her own father, too.
And when her son and his wife divorced,
She raised their children.
Now most everyone she cared for is dead
Or grown and gone;
It's them she talks about.
Everything else—the weather, the daily news—
Leads up to "my Richard this, my Peggy that."
She tries to bring them back by talking about them.
People say, "Who wants to hear that old biddy Emily
Yackety-yack about her family?"
Comfort her, God; send memories of those she cared for
To people her loneliness.

Give her a sense of their presence, and of Yours,
And give me
The strength to listen
When she chatters on and on.

This Changing World

They say old people hate change, and in a way that's right
    because change usually means our being worse off.
Less money. A furnished room instead of a house. Di-
    minished strength. Fewer friends.
On the other hand, new things are fun and I think we
    marvel over them more than the young.
Born without television, it seems a miracle to us.
Buildings of reflecting glass make us catch our breath,
    computers dazzle us.
If we're lucky, we have a friend, more or less
    Our own age, to whom we can say:
    "Can you beat that?"
And the next day somebody always does.

Snow

The snow is so beautiful, God.
It turns the marsh grass
Into plumed scepters,
Bends the pine low,
Frosts the hedge.
The sky is the color of the inside of a shell,
A lone duck flies by
With a sense of urgency.
Ice floes drift on a pewter sea,
And new snow falls,
Silently.
Oh, God, how can I bear to die
And leave Your lovely earth?

Come to Think of It

Meaning no offense, God, but if I were doing it,
I'd let people be old first and get it over with
And have their youth to look forward to.
Browning calls old age "the last of life for which the first
    was made."
I don't buy that.
I give You credit for having something better in mind.
Whenever I start wondering what that could be,
My mind keeps coming back
To the impossible possibility:
Eternal life.

Looking Back

I have been young, and now am old

Psalms 37:25

I Don't Hear as Well
as I Used To

I don't hear as well as I used to, God,
People have to shout and repeat things.
Frankly, a lot of what they have to say
Isn't worth repeating,
And the world's too noisy anyway.
The important thing is, I can hear,
Not with my ears, but with my heart,
What I really want to:
The children, when they were little,
Saying "I love you, Mama."
Dan, when we lost all our savings,
Saying "Hold me, Anne."
Stephen in front of all those people,
Saying "My mother should be receiving this honor
Instead of me."
My father-in-law, dying, laying his hand on my hair,
"You're a good gel, Annie. Carry on."
It's no fun going deaf,
But there are worse things,
And I do have a lot of good memories
To listen to.

For Parents and Poets
and the Aurora Borealis

"DEAR ABBY: a mother wrote saying she was "AT WITS END" because her 30-year-old widowed daughter let her housekeeping go while she did "useless" things like writing

poetry, planting flowers, taking ballet lessons. And she dragged her six-year-old son to museums and art exhibits. ("What can a six-year-old learn from an art exhibit?" she asks.)

I endorse your reply in which you defended the daughter, and would like to add that my parents "dragged" me to concerts, museums, and art exhibits when I was a toddler.

I was awakened one night to "come see the Northern Lights" and told of the Aurora Borealis. I saw Sousa in one of his last concerts, and heard Mark Twain in his last appear-

ance in his native state. I was reading at the age of four, and soon afterwards my father opened his entire library to me showing me how to handle books carefully—they were precious.

Abby, I bless my parents for showing me the beauty of the world. I continue to find life interesting and exciting. I am 79."

AMEN.

For My Mother-in-Law
in Heaven

I think of her often,
My mother-in-law, long dead now.
I wish I'd had time to get to know her better.
She could have taught me a lot
About animals and birds,
About the sea,
About how to bring up boys,
Because, of course, what she was and did
Had a lot to do with how my husband turned out.
I wish I could thank her
For teaching him to be truthful and kind,
Courageous and just.
I wonder if she and I will meet in the hereafter.
Will there be a hereafter?
Nowadays in church they don't talk much about heaven
They way they did when I was a girl.
They don't argue about whether or not
We'll recognize our loved ones,
They don't talk about death as a door
With everyone who has died before us on the other side.
My husband, who has a lot more education
Than I have, says that the plan
(if there is one and he thinks not)
Is not likely to be that simple.
He chooses his words carefully,
Doesn't say "impossible" or "silly,"

Though knowing him as well as I do,
I'm inclined to think those were the words that came
First to his mind.
Now that death is such an imminent possibility
For both of us
I find myself longing
For survival of personality,
Wishing we could spend eternity with those we've loved,
With those who have loved us,
With those we've never had a chance to love.
Some people say that if You are, as I believe You are,
The God of all universes,
You must have some more sweeping plan,
Yet I keep hoping survival of the self we most deeply are
Is part of it.
My husband says, what will be will be.
He's more accepting,
In reality, more religious,
Though only You and I would say so.
I'll certainly be careful not to breathe the word.
Agnostics hate to be called religious,
Especially when they're praying.
His mother was the same way.
I think of her often.

Bachelor

My friend had bad luck with his children.
His son wouldn't follow his profession,
Sits in the woods making pots.
His daughter married and divorced,
Brings her two children home to Mama,
Runs around.
The youngest boy wouldn't get a job
Because he wants to be a big rock star.
He wants his father to give him money for equipment,
To make a film and what all I don't know.
They fight.
A man like me, has no children,
Gets to thinking he's missing something.
Then he listens to his friends
And finds out what he's missing:
Trouble.

Occupational Therapy

Preserve me from the occupational therapist, God,
She means well, but I'm too busy to make baskets.
I want to relive a day in July
When Sam and I went berrying.
I was eighteen,
My hair was long and thick
And I braided it and wound it round my head
So it wouldn't get caught on the briars,
But when we sat down in the shade to rest
I unpinned it and it came tumbling down,
And Sam proposed.
I suppose it wasn't fair
To use my hair to make him fall in love with me,
But it turned out to be a good marriage,
And years later when our daughter said
She thought she'd cut her hair,
I said, "Oh don't. There's something
Mystical about long hair. If after a year
You still want to cut it, do, but think it
Over." A year later,
She said, "Oh Mom, I'm so glad you told me not to cut
     my hair,
Jeff loves it so."
Oh, here she comes, the therapist, with scissors and paste.
Would I like to try decoupage?
"No," I say, "I haven't got time."

"Nonsense," she says, "you're going to live a long, long
    time."
That's not what I mean,
I mean that all my life I've been doing things
For people, with people, I have to catch up
On my thinking and feeling.
About Sam's death, for one thing.
At the time there were so many things to do,
So many people around,
I had to keep assuring everyone I'd be all right,
I had to eat and make sure they noticed,
So they wouldn't keep coming to see me when
They had other things to do.
I had to comfort the children
And Sam's old friends who got scared
(If Sam could die, they could die, too).
I had to give his clothes away and pay the bills,
I didn't have time to think about how brave he was,
How sweet. One day,
Close to the end, I asked if there was anything I could do,
He said, "Yes, unpin your hair."
I said, "Oh, Sam, it's so thin now and gray."
"Please," he said, "unpin it anyway."
I did and he reached out his hand—
The skin transparent, I could see the blue veins—
And stroked my hair.
If I close my eyes, I can feel it. Sam.
"Please open your eyes," the therapist says,
"You don't want to sleep the day away."
As I say, she means well,
She wants to know what I used to do,

| 47

Knit? Crochet?
Yes, I did all those things,
And cooked and cleaned
And raised five children,
And had things happen to me.
Beautiful things, terrible things,
I need to think about them,
At the time there wasn't time,
I need to sort them out,
Arrange them on the shelves of my mind.
The therapist is showing me glittery beads,
She asks if I might like to make jewelry.
Her eyes are as bright as the beads,
She's a dear child and she means well,
So I tell her I might
Some other day.

Grandfather's Clock

God, thank You for arranging it so that I have
In my old age something I've always wanted:
A grandfather's clock.
It keeps me company,
Gives me a sense of family
(It was my husband's mother's),
I even like the necessity of winding it.
There's continuity in chores that must be done
At a certain time.
Now that nobody needs me anymore
I might get the day and night mixed up,
Not bother to get up.
But the clock on the stair reminds me,
Bongs out the hours with dignity.
We've seen the same things, the clock and I,
Birthdays, quarrels, death.
My David used to wind it.
Now, when I wind it, I think of him.
You gave me a good husband, God.
I don't really deserve
A grandfather's clock, too.

The Black Night

The darkness deepens, Lord, with me abide.

HYMN

Nowhere to Go but Old

I'm old
And I'm going to get older.

O my God,
Seriously,
It just hit me.
All along I've been acting as if old age were the flu,
Or a sprained ankle,
Painful, inconvenient, but something I'd get over.
Which is not a bad way to act.
But I can't act that way any more.
Because I'm suddenly struck, laid low, weighed down
With the truth.
I'm old and I'm going to get older.
There is no alternative.
There is nothing that can be done about it.
So I don't have to look for alternatives.
I don't have to try to do something about it.
A liberating thought,
If you look at it that way.
Help me to look at it that way.
Help me to rejoice in the freedom of letting You run the
    show.

Escape Plan

I'm reading about a seventy-two-year-old woman who ran
    away
From a nursing home very like this one.
I play with the idea, try it on,
How would it feel to do that?
Glorious, I know. But could I accomplish it?
Where would I go? And would it be right?
It would frighten the children,
Make them feel guilty. Still and all,
I gave so many years to them,
Don't I deserve what's left of my life?
It's not just that I'm not happy here,
I'm not alive. I grow more passive every day.
I don't know if they tranquilize me
(when I flush my medication down the toilet
the fog seems to go out of my head; of course,
I also have more pain) but being treated like a child
Makes you childlike. Dependent. Whatever spunk I had
Seems to be withering away, like an Indian fakir
Who refuses to use his arm until it's useless.
Is it too late? Will they find me and bring me back?
Not if I plan carefully.
I'll need money. And a friend on the outside to help.
O God, bless this venture. Forgive me
If it brings anyone distress. You did, after all,
Lead the children of Israel out of Egypt
Into the wilderness. Lead me.

I'm Lonely

I'm lonely.

I'm lonely, but I don't dare say so.

My friends and relatives fret enough as is. They don't want me to live alone. They keep saying, aren't you lonely? And I keep saying no. Because I'm not lonely in the way they mean.

I'm lonely for people who were and are no more.

I'm lonely for one person most of all.

I'm lonely for the ways things were. When the children were little and depended on me. I miss their need. I miss being at the center of life instead of out here on the edge.

Going to live with one of the children, going into a home, is no answer to my kind of loneliness. But You, O Lord, are.

Life Is So Eventless

I forget what day it is because one day is like another.
They're gray and run together like oatmeal.
I'm bored and it makes me cranky. I feel like a child kept
    indoors on a rainy day, whining "What can I do
    now?"
Only now there is no patient mother to suggest finger-
    painting or a tea party for the dollls.
All right, I'll be mother and child. I'll suggest things I can
    do.
Have a tea party for a friend. Surely I can think of one
    person who'll come. We'll talk about things that are
    happening to other people. In the world. I'd better
    read the newspaper so I'll know. I'll use the good
    spoons. An event.
I could even—don't laugh—fingerpaint. Crazy idea, but
    why not?
I can almost feel the paint squishing through my fingers.
An event. No, an invent.
Help me invent events.
You didn't mean life to be oatmeal.

Pain

Pain isolates,
No matter how many friends you have
Or how devoted.
Well-meaning, they sit beside your bed,
And press your hand,
You slip away,
Though your fingers stay entwined.
I have gone into the pain, deep and far,
How cold, how desolate it is here,
Starting at every sound,
Half hoping, half in fear,
Death, is that you?
Now, are you here?

Nostalgia

Men are climbing ladders with strings of lights
To decorate the Christmas tree
In the square.
It occurs to me to stop and watch
But I do not.
I hurry by.
I must get up my courage before I dare
Take a chance. Nostalgia
Is a two-edged sword,
The joy of remembering
Is as sharp as the pain,
Comes when I least expect it,
Cuts me to ribbons.
Strange, when the young speak of aging,
They use words like mellow.
They imagine memory to be a soft amber glow,
When, in reality, You and I know,
It is more like a laser beam.

Give me courage to look at what was, is, and is to be,
The blazing radiance of Your Face.

Isolation

Songbirds cannot sing in isolation.
No bird can. Neither can any human being.
But we are not alone.
You are with us.
Even here. In the nursing home.
I can talk to You.
You can talk to me.
And You can lead me
Out of myself,
To make contact with Your world,
Even if the only person I see all day
Is the nurse who brings me my tray.
I can find out about her,
What she looks forward to,
What she's afraid of.
I can read. There are people in books.
I can write letters.
And I can try to move away from my self-centeredness
Closer to You.
Birds cannot sing in isolation.
But we are not alone.

I Hate the Way I Look

I *mind* being wrinkled
And stooped and
Shaky and
Gray.
When I look in the mirror,
I feel betrayed. As if
A dear friend had turned into an ugly beast.
But that's unfair.
My body is still my friend.
It struggles valiantly to do my bidding.
I should be kinder to it.
The years have been pelting it and I haven't helped much.
I eat too much, drink too much, get angry too much,
    overwork.
Actually, my body
Has forgiven me a lot.
I should be more charitable to it now.
When young people look away in distaste, I
Should say: Never mind, old friend-body,
They don't know all you've been through.
When they're old one day, too,
I just hope they take it as well as you.

Suffering

It's sleeting, my feet are wet,
I'm cold, my coat's too thin,
Once I had a fur coat,
Beaver, sleek and fine,
My initials embroidered in the satin lining.
But that was long ago
Before John died.
I'm glad he can't see me now,
Thick and slow,
In this old sweater and coat.
I had the slimmest waist,
I used to tie ribbons around it
And let them blow behind me when I danced.
"Like a butterfly," John said,
Catching me, kissing me.
Oh, we had such fun
When we were young,
And for a long time after,
No babies, which was sad,
But a lot of laughter.
Whatever we did, we did together.
Now he's gone,
And here I am, no overshoes, walking through the snow.
But I have a warm room waiting,
A hot plate to make tea on.
I'm so much better off than the old ladies I see

Huddled in the subway, in arcades and lobbies.
"Crazy," people say,
As if that makes suffering less.
I've never understood suffering, God,
Never been able to make any sense of it,
I only know that hard as things are for me now,
Others are so much worse off.
Help them, God.
Help me to be grateful for what I have,
Help me to see the beauty of the snow
Whirling against the lamplight,
In a halo,
Help me understand
That it is not necessary for me
To understand
Suffering. My job is to endure
Without bitterness,
And to care and share.

In the Middle
of the Night

O God, if You are up there, out there, in here,
I yearn to say, "Give me a sign."
I've been taught not to ask for signs,
But so much of what I've been taught
Has turned out to be untrue.
I know I should have faith,
Shouldn't question,
Shouldn't doubt,
But however hard I tried,
Could I hide from You
This desperate screaming ache to ask,
Do You exist?
Will I
When I have died?

Ideals

I thought when I grew old, I'd grow
Philosophical.
People expect you to.
Viewing life from a lofty perspective
Would be a help.
Instead, trifles loom large,
There being little else of importance happening.
Worst of all, I seem to be missing
A lot of my old ideals.
Help me find them again, God.
Or help me find new ones.
I haven't worked out a real philosophy yet
And maybe I never will.
I don't know.
I do know that a couple of worthwhile ideals
Are a big help getting up mornings.

My Eyes Are Failing

For quite a while now, I've been pretending.
That it was just that I was tired,
That the light was bad.
But my eyes really are getting worse.
I'm afraid to go to the doctor because I'm afraid of what
he'll say.
Which is silly. Either there is something to be done. Or
there is not.
If it's glasses, hallelujah, and help me find the money. If
it's an operation, see me through. If I am going blind,
hold me. Help me put down the terror that rises in
my gut at the word.
Blind. There. I've said it. The ghost word that has been
haunting me.
Help me remember, if I have to walk in the dark, that I
have had a lot of years of seeing clean and clear. I
know the slender shape of a birch tree. I know the
color of irises and dawn. I have seen thousands and
thousands of things in my life, I can conjure them in
my mind's eye.
No matter what happens, I shall not be without beautiful
sights.
It is just that I may have to settle for the ones I have al-
ready seen.

I Don't Know
What's Going to Happen

I don't know what's going to happen
And I'm afraid.

I might fall and break my hip and never walk again.
I might become senile and be a burden to everyone.
The money might run out.
I might have a stroke and wake up with one side of my
    face sagging.
I see these things happening all around me.
There seems to be no end to them.
And no end to the horror show that goes on behind my
    eyes if I let it.
Help me not to let it.
Help me not to look ahead but to this day, this hour, this
    minute.
If the present is difficult, help me cope with it.
If it is painful, help me bear it.
If it is empty, help me fill it.
If it is good, help me enjoy it.
Most of all, help me live it.

I'm a Coward

O God, I can't do it,
Go through what has to come,
Bear bravely what has to be borne.
I hate self-pity, but You know
I have no courage, although
Everybody thinks I have.
I've used props. What will happen when they're gone?
My husband. Not a day goes by but what the mere
Fact of his existence quells my panic,
To say nothing of its very real hand on my hair,
His joking way of putting things in perspective.
If anything happens to him, I'll go to pieces.
And, of course, I'm vain.
I pretend I don't care about looks, but You know
How whenever I have to face some situation I'm afraid of,
I look in the mirror and think, "Well, they can't be too
    hard on you if you're a little pretty."
Which really is true. What will I do
When I'm altogether ugly? How can I go out
On the cruel streets? And what will I do
When I'm imprisoned in a bed or a chair? I've always been
    impatient.
I can't tell anybody these things because they think I'm
    strong,
They don't know I'm a coward. You do.
Is that why You gave me a husband, a little prettiness,

70 |

Good health for so long? Propping me up like a spindly
     plant,
Waiting for me to grow strong?
Can I have a little longer, God? Thank You for Your care.
And when You take the props away, please, please stand
Very near.

In the Way

I feel I'm in the way.
Nonsense, I *am* in the way,
Though the family tells me I'm not.
No sense priding myself in not making demands.
They have to help me dress, bathe, follow the
    conversation.
They have to take me to the doctor.
They can't leave me alone without worrying.
And they have to look at me and see, beyond the ugliness
    of my wrinkled face and wavering hands, the specter
    of their own deterioration.
The young people, of course, don't believe they will ever
    be old.
But I am often an embarrassment to them.
They try to remember the way I used to be and pay hom-
    age to that.
They don't know that I am here, imprisoned in old age,
    trying to make contact with the world.
What can I do, Lord? What should I do?
I love them and long to communicate with them and can-
    not bear to be in the way.
Is there something You can teach them through me?
Is there something You want me to learn?
Help me, Lord, to understand why I am still here.

Bad News

Bad news.
A lot of it
All at once.
It feels like a blow,
I stagger, reel,
My eyes blur,
I'm frightened,
And I must confess, God
I feel outraged.
How could You do this to me,
After all I've been through,
Now when I'm already so low,
It's not sporting to hit a fellow when he's down.
I know, it's not sporting to whine, either.
I'm behaving like a child.
After all these years I ought to know
How foolish it is to ask: Why me?
For centuries men have been shouting at the heavens:
Why me? Why me?
And other men have invented reasons.
All wrong.
There is no reason beyond
My ways are not Your ways.
The only thing to do is accept that and go on.
Help me to.
It's hard.
And I'm afraid.

I'm Disgusted with My Life

O God, I'm disgusted with my life.
Some people seem to do everything right.
I did everything wrong.
Quit school. Took the first job that came along.
Married because everybody else was,
To be a man, not a boy.
Wrong. Found that out pretty soon,
We both did. But by that time
We had the kids to bring up,
Drag up, I should say, pull and haul it was.
All the way. Now they're off doing their own thing
And the old lady's dead and I'm ready to live
But my life's used up.
Practically. Actually, I'm still here,
More or less in one piece,
Thinking these thoughts, imagining You hear,
Imagining You saying, "Here's a day.
Wanna make something of it?"
Okay, God, I get the message.

For a Son

O God, my son's wife left him and he is distraught
And I am powerless to help.
What can I say?
That there will be another girl someday?
There will, of course, but he can't believe that now.
Now he is destroying himself,
He may lose his job,
He may even kill himself.
I know You gave Your Son to save us,
But my son's agony seems to serve no purpose.
It was a good, productive marriage,
The girl's torn up, too.
If I could take their pain, I would.
My life's almost through,
It is no longer necessary for me to be happy.
For everything there is said to be a price.
What can I pay, what sacrifice can I make,
What can I do or say to roll this stone of suffering away
From my beloved son? Only You, O God, can help.
O God, help.
He's a good boy.

Now That She's Gone

There's not much to come home to
Now that she's gone.
I keep forgetting,
Sort of expecting her to be there
Like always.
So when I open the door
The silence hits me
Like a fist,
Knocks the wind out of me.
I'm glad there's nobody there to see.
They'd send me up like a kook.
But
The air inside the house is hard and cold
And it used to be warm and soft
With her talking,
Saying nothing,
Asking silly questions—
"Is that you?" she'd ask,
And I'd say, "No, it's Santa Claus,"
Or "the man-in-the-moon,"
But I felt like me
Then.
A lot of the time now I don't.

Losses

Today I read about a man who slashed his wrists because
    he lost his hat.
He was old, and of course, they say he was crazy.
I think not.
I think he'd just had all the losses he could take.
He said as much.
His last words were, "O God, now I've lost my hat, too."
I know how he felt.
Every time you turn around, time—with a little help from
    your friends—grabs off something else. Something
    precious. At least to you.
Hearing. Sight. Beauty. Job. House. Even the corner gro-
    cery turns into a parking lot and is lost.
Finally, you lose the thing you can't do without—hope
    (that it can get better).
Dear God, when he gets to heaven, let that man find his
    hat on the gatepost.

The Courage of Friends

*I prefer to strive in bravery with the bravest,
rather than in wealth with the wealthiest, or in
greed with the greediest.*

PLUTARCH,
Lives: Marcus Cato. Ch X, Sec 4

What a new face courage puts on everything!
RALPH WALDO EMERSON,
Letters and Social Aims

Flu

Oh, wow, Lord,
This flu bug, this virus
Has hit me hard,
Laid me low.
Scares me, too,
Because at my age when you get knocked down,
You don't know if you'll ever get up.
Well, nobody ever knows that
Or knows for sure anything that's going to happen.
All we do know is that a lot of the happening is up to us.
Take my friend Wilhemina Gray,
Broke her hip at eighty, and they say
When you break a hip,
That's i.t. It.
But Billie's up and around and walking without a limp.
Have to laugh at the way she tells it.
Seems she went out in the middle of the night,
Five below, in her nightgown and slippers
Because she heard this cat meowing and she was afraid it
    would freeze.
There's this concrete walk beside Billie's house
And it was all ice and down she went,
Splat. Arms and legs every which way. Felt like every-
    thing broke.
well, she figgered, this is the end. Tomorrow or the day
    after

(She couldn't remember which)
The milkman would come with his every-other-day
Delivery of cream for the cats
And find her there.
"Frozen solid," she said,
"Like the ice maiden." (Billie's a reader.)
So she folded her hands over her breast,
Which isn't much but she's pretty all the same,
And waited to freeze,
When all of the sudden, she heard this voice:
"Get up, you damn fool.
You may not be able to,
But you can try."
So she tried and made it
And we've had some good times since.
Of course, I asked Billie about the voice,
Whose voice was it, swearing and rough?
"Mine," Billie said.
"I didn't recognize it, either,
But it was mine."
Well, I live alone, too, and I better not depend on voices.
Better set the alarm clock
To tell me when to take the pills.
I'll take aspirin and juices, too.
This flu shall pass (Hey, that's a good one. When I'm bet-
    ter, I'll tell it to Billie).

Weather

I called a friend today.
She lives in an inland city
In a house that gets hot as a furnace
On dog days like this.
"Isn't the heat awful?" I said.
She said, "Oh no. It's good for my hip. I
   haven't had a twinge of pain since this hot spell began."
She says cold weather is invigorating
And rain on the roof "sings her to sleep."
She "just loves" the snow,
And fog, "Oh, fog is lovely—so gentle, you know."
I asked her, "If you could choose any weather,
What weather would you choose?"
She said, "Next Monday."
"What?" I asked. "How can you possibly know what
      Monday's weather will be?"
"I don't," she said. "Don't you see? That's the fun of it.
I *like* God to choose
And then have Him
Surprise me."

A Beautiful House

So often, God, You work Your miracles
Behind the scenes
And we see only
The tip of the iceberg.
I'm thinking of my friend Ellen.
No education,
Hardly ever reads.
Yesterday, she took me to see
"A beautiful house."
A renovation,
Done not by her son
(I could understand that)
But by some kids she barely knows.
"They took the old Lambeth house, Rose,"
She said, "and completely redid it.
Isn't it beautiful?"
Crazy roofline, used lumber unpainted,
Plexiglass bubbles,
Found objects in the yard,
Iron pipe railing,
Greenery in pots,
Marijuana?
"The girl," Ellen said, "makes those pots,
Throws them on a wheel.
She let me try my hand at it.
I love the feel of the wet slip,

I may become a potter in my old age."
She's seventy-nine.
Where, Lord, and when and how
Did she learn or grow enough to know
The house *is* beautiful
Sitting there among stern Colonials?
(The neighbors are outraged.)
Help me to grow, too.
Help me enlarge
My ability to accept
Approve
Appreciate
The unprecedented,
Upsetting,
Beautiful ideas of the young.

Grandchildren

The grandchildren haven't turned out the way we thought they would. Their parents, my children, are hurt and angry, ashamed and worried about it. I'm not. To tell you the truth, I like these kids. The way they are. Open and honest. Disorganized and gentle. Scruffy and kind. They don't seem to mind spending time with me. We talk about real things. Dreams. Peace. The sky. They tell me living is more important than accomplishing things. I agree.

Their parents are outraged by this kind of talk, so I don't go into it. I just say, "The kids came." The parents say, "That's good; at least they have a sense of duty."

I think they have a sense of love.

Letter to Thomas B. Russiano

A Letter to the Editor:
I'm a part-time college student, and I made a remark in a class to the effect that I agree with the Women's Liberation Movement. One of the students who knew my age (I am 76) said, for the benefit of all, that at his age he was still chasing women. I answered that I was not trying to catch any women, nor was I trying to chase any away. What I was doing was following them—for they are the only group on the horizon today heading toward a better world, and that is why I am giving them my wholehearted support.

Thomas B. Russiano
Brownsville, Texas

Dear God:

I trust
You will see to it that
Thomas B. Russiano of Brownsville, Texas
Gets an A.

Dear Mr. Russiano, or may I call you Tom:
Shall we dance?

Lost and Found

Every once in a while
I lose my eyeglasses
And my zest for life.
But I find them again.
It's always Mary who points them out
Some funny way so as not to make me feel a fool.
She'll say,
"Those aphids are getting away with murder."
And I'll find my glasses in the garage
Next to the insecticide spray,
And end up gardening all day,
And planning to dig up a vegetable bed tomorrow.
We don't talk about it but I hope she knows
I'd be lost without her funny little ways
Of helping me find things like my glasses
And a meaning to my days.
Thanks, God, for giving me this wife.

For Pluck

I read a letter in the newspaper from a lady who signed herself "Gram" and said she was seventy-three. She has learned, she said, one helpful hint about how to live with a fractured arm, with a cast to the elbow. Slide a stocking wide top first over the cast to keep it clean and to make it easier to get your coat on. Snip out the toe so you can move your fingers. One more bit of advice from Gram: Don't climb on kitchen chairs!

O Gram. You plucky lucky lady.
To take a broken arm at seventy-three as a matter of
    course.
No self-pity. Only ingenuity. And the impulse to help
    others in the same pickle. And humor. That warning
    about the chair. What were you doing up on it? Tak-
    ing down curtains? Putting up pictures?
God love you, Gram.
Which, of course, He does.
I do, too.

My Husband
of So Many Years

How good he is,
My husband of so many years;
Tears come to my eyes
When I see how crepey his neck has become,
How bravely he tries
To straighten up.
Once his jaw was hard and he stood tall
With no effort;
It is as if his body had been sabotaged
One dark night
By some unseen enemy,
I know he feels that way.
Yet when I look at him today
I feel far more tender toward him
Than ever I did when he was young and strong
And seemingly invulnerable.
O my dear old friend-lover,
Time-ravaged fellow-traveling
Camouflaged boy,
Can it help you to know,
Can it help you to hear,
That not only as you were but as you are
You are to me
Inexpressibly dear.

Looking Up

*But they that wait upon the Lord shall renew their
strength.*

Isaiah 40:31

Come, captain age,
With your sea chest full of treasure!
Under the yellow and wrinkled tarpaulin
Disclose the carved ivory
And the sandalwood inlaid with pearl
Riches of wisdom and years.

SARAH N. CLEGHORN,
"Come, Captain Age"

Real Christmas

The week after Christmas, in a strange town,
I went walking to clear my head of holiday confusion.
I passed a church,
The door was open,
Rare nowadays when everything seems to be locked tight
Against vandalism and theft.
I walked by, then turned back and went in.
Somehow, because Christmas was over, I expected to see
The church clean and bare
But it was filled with poinsettias and greens,
Candles ablaze, a Mexican creche on the altar,
The Christmas tree was lighted.
Suddenly real Christmas happened for me
As it has not for years and years.
In the stillness I felt a stirring of hope,
The world was old and tired like me
When You sent Your infant Son to say:
"Behold, all things are made new."

Hope

Maybe I'll sneak through,
Squeak by,
Conk out before the real horrors of old age
Catch up with me.
Does everybody think this way
About themselves?
Is it wrong? Right?
Foolish? Wise?
Will I come a cropper and be worse off
For having got my hopes up?
Or is hope worth having
For however long it lasts?
Maybe as the kids say,
"You gotta believe,
Wishing will make it so,"
And so forth.
I don't know.
But I figure to play it that way.

Adventure

"Like a good many people who are in or above their seventies, Mother had far more courage and curiosity than fear."

I read that in a book recently and I thought, it's true. While I'm still too afraid too often, I've shed a lot of my fears. I worry less. I used to think this or that action could affect my whole life. Well, most of my life is behind me now, and what's ahead probably won't be worth sacrificing current adventure for.

Like the man said. "Do you want to live forever?"

I don't know about that; I do know I want to live for real. So when I hesitate, I tell myself: You have hardly anything to lose.

So open the door. Ask the question. Accept the invitation. Get on the bus. Try it. Go alone.

Climb. Plunge. Explore.

For Music

Thanks, God, for music.
It isn't illegal or immoral or fattening or even too expen-
    sive.
And you don't have to be young to enjoy it.
In fact, I'm only now beginning to enjoy it fully.
When I was younger I had too many things to do.
And I spent the time in between planning more activities.
Now I have time.
And I am lifted up and carried away and lightened and
    brightened with the magic and majesty.
Thanks, God, for making a world which contains music,
for making men who have the talent and desire to create
    it, for giving me ears to hear and leisure to listen.

A Place of My Own

I like tidying up this place, Lord,
Sweeping up, wiping the sink,
Making the faucets shine.
It's not all that grand of a place, Lord,
But thank the Lord, Lord, it's mine.
It upsets my children to see me here.
"You don't have to live like this, Pop.
Live with one of us," they say.
"There's room. We'd love to have you."
What can I say?
I sound stubborn, ungrateful,
But I don't want to leave this place.
I'm lonely, sure. But there's nothing they can do about
    that.
Now that Margaret's gone and they're all grown.
Having a place of my own,
Snug as a ship's cabin, helps.
It's comforting. And You'll be here with me, Lord,
If, as they keep saying, "something happens."
What do they mean "if"? When.

I Can Walk

I can walk and it's wonderful.
I can't walk as fast as I used to.
Or as far.
But the countryside is as beautiful as ever:
Flowering trees,
Snowfields,
Hills, brooks, sky.
The smells still startle and exhilarate:
Woodsmoke,
Honeysuckle, wet leaves, pine.
And funny things still happen along the way;
Today a young girl stopped her bicycle to ask,
"Is this a bicycle pump?" I told her yes,
And showed her how to use it.
Then a middle-aged couple stopped their car
And said there used to be a restaurant near here
With an Indian on the sign, did I remember it?
I did, but it was torn down years ago. I told them so.
They said, "We thought you'd know."
They meant they thought I was old enough to know.
Well, I am. Old enough to know a lot of things—
Like how wonderful it is to be able to get out and walk.
Thank you, God.

For Warmth

Thanks, God, for warmth.
For the sun coming up like hope,
Like joy in the morning,
Laying a gentle hand on my hair,
Melting the sharpness of the world.
Thanks, God, for warmth.
For warm clothes, warm rooms,
A warm bed.
For warm-bodied animals. Cats. Dogs.
Warm water to wash in,
Tea, soup, warm bread,
A fire on the hearth,
Warm friendships,
Kindness from a stranger.
Thanks, God, for warmth.
It feels like Your smile.

Sales Manager

What a relief not to have to be
Up and at 'em all the time.
As You know, I used to be a human dynamo
In business.
"Grab your hat, here comes Joe."
Everybody said, "He'll hate retirement."
I let 'em think so.
Secretly I was scared I'd have a heart attack or something
Before I'd gone the distance.
Thanks, God, for letting me make it.
And between You and me and the lamppost,
Waking up in the morning without a sales quota to meet
Is like being in heaven already.

The Park

Visiting in the city, I took a walk
And found a park,
Small, a single block,
A plaque said it was a gift,
In Memoriam.
God, how good of You to incline
The minds of men
To memorialize
Loved ones in such a loving way.
Tired office workers sat
Turning pale faces to the sun.
There were young lovers and a few
Young mothers with babies bouncing in strollers
Or sweetly asleep,
And there were old people like me,
Nodding and smiling,
Enjoying the fountain,
The ivy,
And the Ginko tree.

Baskets

I bought a basket today
In a big department store,
I brought it home to my city room
Where it smells of country meadows,
Or I imagine it does.
It reminds me how wide Your world is,
How flowers grow by the fieldful,
How clever the fingers of man are,
How themes run through the ages,
Egyptians, Mayans, Hungarians, Sioux,
Making baskets, plaiting straw,
Weaving reeds, and now
My granddaughter, eighteen,
Writing from her fancy Eastern college:
"I'm taking a course
In basketry."

Creation

Lemons,
Fuchsias,
Orioles,
Hickory nuts.
If there can be
Such scent, shape, color, intricacy,
There has to be
A God.
Why has it taken me so many years
To reach this conclusion?

Driving

I'm not as young as I'd like to be but
I've got my health,
My eyesight,
Most of my marbles,
And an old rattletrap of a car.
I'm so glad I can still drive.
Days on end, the old jalopy sits in the driveway
And I don't go anywhere,
But just knowing I could
Feels good.
I might want the paper, say, or an ice cream.
Gotta watch the gas, of course,
And I can't afford any big trips,
But just tooling around town is fun.
Sometimes I turn on the radio and sing along
At the top of my lungs. No one to hear
And think I'm queer.
Sometimes I park and watch kids playing ball,
Ducks in a pond,
Guys loading stuff onto flatcars down at the rail yards,
Sunset. Funny thing to be praying about—a car—
But I do want to thank You, God
For my car, for being able to drive it,
For the interesting things I see,
For feeling free.

A Beautiful Dress

A friend said, "That's a beautiful dress."
And I said, "Thank you."
I should have said, "Thank God."
For giving me a beautiful dress.
For color and line and texture.
For eyes to see and fingers to feel.
For a friend to notice
My beautiful dress.

Golf Course

I walked past the golf course this evening,
Dusk,
Sprinklers on,
White white against green green,
Stone wall,
I put my hand on it,
Warm from the sun,
Insect hum,
Good wet grass smell,
Couple of hippie types
Knocking balls around,
Shoulders easy, easy with each other,
Easy with the world,
Not trying to win,
Just enjoying the evening,
Now that the corporation kings
And their wives,
In proper golf attire,
Have gone.
Once I'd have been outraged,
What are they doing here? They're
Not members. Now,
I watch and smile and lean into the moment.
I don't even feel bad that I don't play anymore.
Club's got too expensive for me
And I don't know anyone,

Most of my friends have retired and moved away.
Some are dead.
I miss the friends and the fun we had,
The rivalry, the jokes,
But somehow in those days, I was never out on the course
At dusk,
Never saw the shadows lengthen,
Never noticed the wild asters against the wall,
Never took time to lean against the wall,
Smiling at bearded young guys
Trespassing.
Hi, they call.
Hi, I call back.
They mean more.
So do I.
But it is enough to say
At the green gold quiet
End of day.

Insights

They,
Psychiatrists,
Psychologists,
The experts,
Keep reinventing the wheel.
I just read where
Studies show
Gazing at water,
Brooks, rivers, the sea,
Is tranquilizing.
Next thing you know
They'll discover that crowds
Make people nervous.
The longer I live,
The more it seems to me
Life is a gigantic Easter egg hunt.
We go running around like crazy,
Hunting for brilliant truths
You've hidden in plain sight.

A Sunny House

I've always wanted to live in a sunny house.
I've lived in so many dark places,
Cramped old cities, mill towns,
Hotel rooms with windows opening on air shafts,
Damp dark places, but we made the best of them,
And finally things worked out.
We bought this sunny house,
Bedroom facing east,
Living room facing south,
Big windows, "Our own solarium," Len said.
He loved the sun as much as I did,
He hardly had time to enjoy the house
Before he died,
He didn't leave much, so I thought,
Of course I'll have to sell the house and go,
But no, the boys paid off the mortgage,
Gave it to me, tied in blue ribbons,
Like a diploma.
And here I am, safe in my sunny house,
Remembering the way they stood on each side of me
At the funeral, their strong young hands
Under my elbows, holding me up.
Later they said, "Do you want to come and live with
One of us? Take an apartment? Or stay here?"
I couldn't believe they'd really listen to me,
I thought they'd say it was impractical,

Which it is,
One old lady rattling around
A big sunny house.
But they listened, really listened,
And finally Billy said,
"You always tried to help us do
What we wanted to do,
It's no big deal if we
Return the favor. Besides,
It's a nice place to visit."
Not that they come all that often,
Their jobs keep them busy,
And Len Junior and his family live so far away,
But that's as it should be,
And I'm safe and cozy here
In my sunny house.
Thanks, God, for giving me sons,
Especially these particular ones.

Give Us This Day
Our Daily Bread

Food's fun, God.
Thanks for making it
And for giving me enough.
If I can't have steak every day,
It's better that way.
Hunger hones appetite,
And scarcity abets festivity.
I remember reading a book about a man and a boy
Celebrating Christmas in a cabin in the wilderness,
Maine, I think it was.
They opened a tinned pudding and set it aflame
And tasted ecstasy.
Help me be grateful and not greedy.
Feed the hungry, Lord.
Forgive my excesses, and
Remind me to share.
You can't want us to spend too much time
Thinking about food and yet
You made so many deliciousnesses:
Melons and pears, oysters and champagne,
Graham crackers and apple butter,
Almonds and cheese.
You must have meant to please us, God.
And You do.

Working

There's a lot of joy in my life, Lord.
But You'd never know it from listening to me
Complaining about what I have too little of:
Money, strength and time,
And having to drag these tired bones to work.
Actually, it's a blessing to have a job
At my age.
To have a place to go when I get up mornings.
I know a lot of people envy me.
The company was good to keep me on
Past retirement. I ought to be
Grateful
And I am.
It's just that every year,
Especially in winter, the idea of staying cozily at home
To make soup, read and tidy up the place
Is more appealing.
It's nonsense, of course, because I couldn't afford
To keep this place without a paycheck.
So what it comes down to is
I wouldn't have a problem
If I weren't
Greedy and lazy.

Worldly Goods

I'm giving away my things
And it turns out to be
As much of an occupation
And as much fun
As collecting them was.
I browse among my friends the way
I used to browse in shops.
I try to decide who should have the cameo
I wore as a bride, who would like
My Chinese vase. I go through closets and drawers
And am amazed at what I find.
So many objects. I am ashamed
To have so much when so many have so little.
Worse still, there are a lot of things I hardly ever use.
This handsome fish poacher, for example.
Hammered copper. It came from France.
I used it once or twice. We thought a meal had to be
Meat and potatoes. The kids know better.
My daughter-in-law, Jill, eats only vegetables and fish.
She says it saves grain for the hungry and is a less aggres-
    sive way
To live. Bless her heart, she is a gentle child,
She'll love this poacher, and my silver napkin rings
(She won't use paper napkins—says she wants no tree
To die to wipe her mouth). It takes forever,
Sorting things, I stop and think about where and when

And I find myself thinking, I may have use for this again.
Nonsense. I don't bake angel food cakes anymore,
Give the pan away. Funny, I thought I'd feel a sense of
    loss
With fewer of my things around.
I don't.
I feel exhilarated, free.
Is this why You told the rich man to sell his goods?
I used to think You meant to help the poor.
I think now Your command
Was meant to help the rich man more.

Graduation

Education, that's the ticket.
I didn't have it, so I didn't get too far,
Still and all, life's been good to me.
I worked, married,
No kids, but my wife's a brick,
Sense of humor, keeps herself nice.
I opened a store with my brother, Leo.
We got along like nobody's business
Though everybody says business
And brothers don't mix, you'll fight.
We never did. The night he died, I felt like
I was splitting apart.
I thought, "I'll die, too."
I almost did.
But his kid wanted to go to medical school
And who was there to see he got there but me?
He graduates on Friday.
A favor, God:
Would you make certain Leo's looking down?

Old Neighborhood

I love this neighborhood, God.
I've lived here so long.
The buildings are old friends.
I feel like nodding to them when I walk by.
I'd better not; they'll lock me up.
It's nice to know where things are:
Flower shop, paper stand.
Of course things change,
The butcher retired
And a couple of kids opened a health food store,
I poked my head in, curious, one day,
And they about pulled me inside,
Made me try granola,
Not bad,
She's pretty, thin, plays the recorder.
There's a new front on the hardware store,
I don't see why they wanted to go and do that,
Looked fine to me the way it was,
But that's me, "old status quo,"
My friend Arthur calls me that,
But he's the same way,
Quite a few of us old fogies in this neighborhood,
We kid each other, josh,
You wouldn't have that in your fancy suburb.
So what if the neighborhood's gettng more and more run
    down,

So am I. This way
I don't stick out like a sore thumb,
I blend in here, I fit.
Thanks, God, for this old neighborhood
And for letting me stay.

Our Secret

Hey, Lord, we have a secret.
Not because I won't tell it or You won't reveal it, but
    because no one will believe it. What I mean is: there
    are some things about being old that are fun.
Yes, fun.
The world gets off your back.
They neglect you.
You don't have to keep up appearances.
So you can go back to the fun of being a child.
Watching a spider spin a web.
Making shadow pictures against the light.
Exploring the back yard as if it were a new country.
Eating applesauce and cream instead of dinner.
Dawdling.
Staying up all night. Counting stars.
Staying home from a dull party to play chess with an old
    friend.
Wearing a funny hat.
Why didn't You tell me that besides all the things I hate
    about being old, there'd be some fun in it, too?
I know. I know.
I wouldn't have believed You.

Walking Home

I was going to take the bus
And then I didn't,
Because I didn't
Have the money.
I mean, I had the money but I didn't
Think I ought to spend it.
The fare's fifty cents now,
Half a dollar,
Half *of* a dollar,
And for someone of my means
(Or lack of means)
That's a lot,
So I said to myself,
"All right, I'll hike."
I wasn't looking forward to it though,
I was a little tired,
And I figured I'd be bored,
Putting one foot in front of the other
Isn't the most interesting thing in the world
When you've gone the route a hundred times
Or more before,
And then You put on that light show, God,
It was beautiful, the sky
All apricot and gold, the trees
Silhouetted,
In the space of an hour,

Light wheeled, danced and was done
And one star shone.
It would be an understatement to say
I'm glad I decided to walk home today,
And if I tried to say anything
About your goodness and glory,
I'd have to shout and sing,
Which I'm not about to do.
Ecstasy is not a thing
Folks understand
In a fellow who happens to be seventy-six,
Which I happen to be.
But God, sometimes, between me and You,
I'm singing-shouting glad to be alive.

Old Lovers

Today I saw an advertisement
In a magazine, a picture of two people,
Old,
Hurrying to meet at a fountain in a park.
I couldn't stop looking,
Misty-eyed at the sweetness of it.
Oh, I know the people in the photograph
Are probably paid models,
But I also know that somewhere
Two people
Dowdy to the world
But beautiful to each other
Are finding each other
And finding the world new,
Are dressing carefully,
Are waiting on a park bench,
Are worrying a little
(No watch to consult)
And then
Relief and joy
As the other appears, hurrying,
"I was late because . . . I was afraid you . . ."
"So was I."
"Silly old geese, aren't we?"
"Yes. But you never know."
"That's right. I'm glad you waited."

"I'm glad you came."

"I saw some geese on the pond. Canada geese. Must have
   been twenty.

Shall we go see them?"

"Oh, yes, let's. I'm glad you like birds."
"I'm glad *you* do. I'll bring my Peterson's and binoculars
   next time."
"Too soon for warblers. But there might be a few early
   birds."
"Looking for worms?"
"Oh, you."
"Is that brooch new?"
"It was my mother's. I haven't worn it for years.
But today
I just got the idea to get it out and polish it
And put it on."
"I think it looks beautiful."
He means to him she looks beautiful.
She knows what he means
And although the day has clouded over
And turned cold
She feels warm.
Bless you, old lovers,
Wherever you are,
And bless You, God, for creating
The marvelous mystery of love.
And thanks for reminding me of it
In Your usual practical way.
Some people see burning bushes.
Other people see magazine ads.

Quiet

The world is so full of things, things, things!
I'm sure we should all be as miserable as kings.
Thank God, God, I can go back to my bare little room
And get away from things on sale,
Loudspeakers, Musak, and my friend Emily-and-her-
      aching back.
You're everywhere, God, I know,
But I tend to lose You in crowds.
Then I go home to my quiet little room
And find You there,
Waiting for me.
I hope
It will be
Like that when I die.

Guide Boat

I ought to sell it
Or give it away, Lord,
My Adirondack guide boat,
Out in the shed,
Up in the rafters.
I go out and stand there looking up at it
Remembering.
Churning streams, glassy lakes,
Pine forests, thick and black,
Quivering aspen,
Deer coming to drink,
Wild iris,
Once I saw yellow water lilies
Far as the eye could see.
I went everywhere in that boat,
Maine, Canada,
Deep into the wild.
Molly went with me
Before the babies came,
I can still see her hair,
Red as a maple leaf,
Flaming ahead of me
In the bow.
It was never the same
After she stopped coming along,
Still, I had to go,

Come the first thaw and something called me.
She'd know and say,
"You've got to get away, Tad, you really do,
The office is no place for a man like you."
So I'd get my gear together,
Makes me smile to think of it,
Flannel shirt, slicker, three pairs of socks,
Hatchet, knife,
Life is sweeter near the bone
And I'm getting weary of the claptrap
I seem to have surrounded myself with.
I've half a mind to take the old boat down
And go,
I know
I'm in no shape,
My hands shake like aspen leaves,
My knees are arthritic,
I'd probably have a heart attack before I'd gone a mile,
But so what, God,
As Patton said, Do you want to live forever?
And what a way to go.

Island

The city's no place to grow old.
Sea, beach, gnarled tree,
Everything here is older than I am,
Was here before I was born,
Will be here when I'm gone.
I don't know why that should comfort me
But it does.
It's good, too, not to have to keep up appearances.
I still shave because I always have,
But it's good to know if one day
I up and don't, the gulls won't
Fly away in disgust. No,
They'll be around as usual for the scraps of
Bread I scatter.
Everything here is used, scraped clean,
Washed or blown away.
In the city, death always seemed an outrage.
Here it seems a simple necessity.
I'm a slow learner, God, but the sea
Is a patient teacher.
Thanks for letting me end my days
Learning.

Night and Your Stars

Night and Your stars
Spread out over me,
The air cold and clear,
The smell of woodsmoke,
Somewhere people are sitting around a fire
And I am out here alone,
Once I'd have worried that idea like
A dog with a bone
Till I was overcome with sadness.
Now so many waves of yearning have already washed
    over me,
I'm unmoved,
I have suffered so many losses,
There are few to fear,
So many matters I used to agonize over
Don't matter anymore,
Getting ahead, being invited,
Fitting in, winning.
It's too late for all that now,
Too late to do much more
Than be out here under the stars
Talking to You,
Friendly and peaceful.

ABOUT THE AUTHOR

Elise Maclay is a graduate of the College of William and Mary, where she edited the campus literary magazine. Her writing has been published in *The New York Times,* and in many national magazines, including *McCall's, Parents' Magazine, The Saturday Evening Post, The Reader's Digest* and *Holiday.* She has been a magazine editor and a book editor, and is the author of the cookbook *Bride's-Eye View of Cooking.*

Mrs. Maclay lives with her husband in Connecticut and is the mother of two grown sons, one of whom took some of the photographs that appear in *Green Winter.*